The Triplet Book for Cello

Part One:

First Position Closed

by Cassia Harvey

CHP233

©2013 by C. Harvey Publications® All Rights Reserved.

www.charveypublications.com - print books & free sheet music blog
www.learnstrings.com - downloadable books & chamber music

The Triplet Book for Cello, Part One

1

Left-Hand Warm-Up

Cassia Harvey

©2013 C. Harvey Publications All Rights Reserved.

2

3

String Crossing

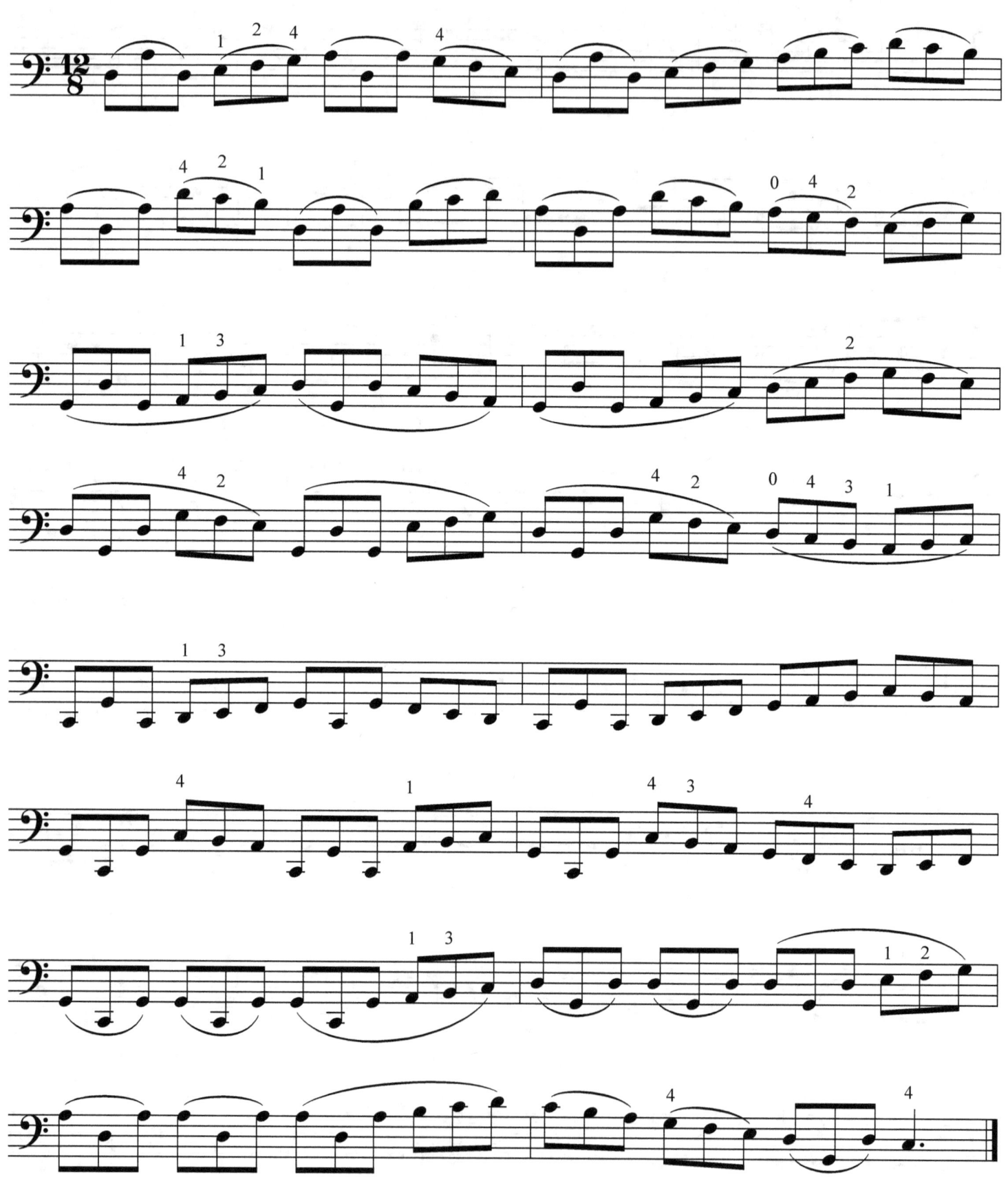

4

The Howlet and the Weazle
Trad., arr. Harvey

Neapolitan Threshers
Trad., arr. Harvey

5

Left-Hand Warm-Up

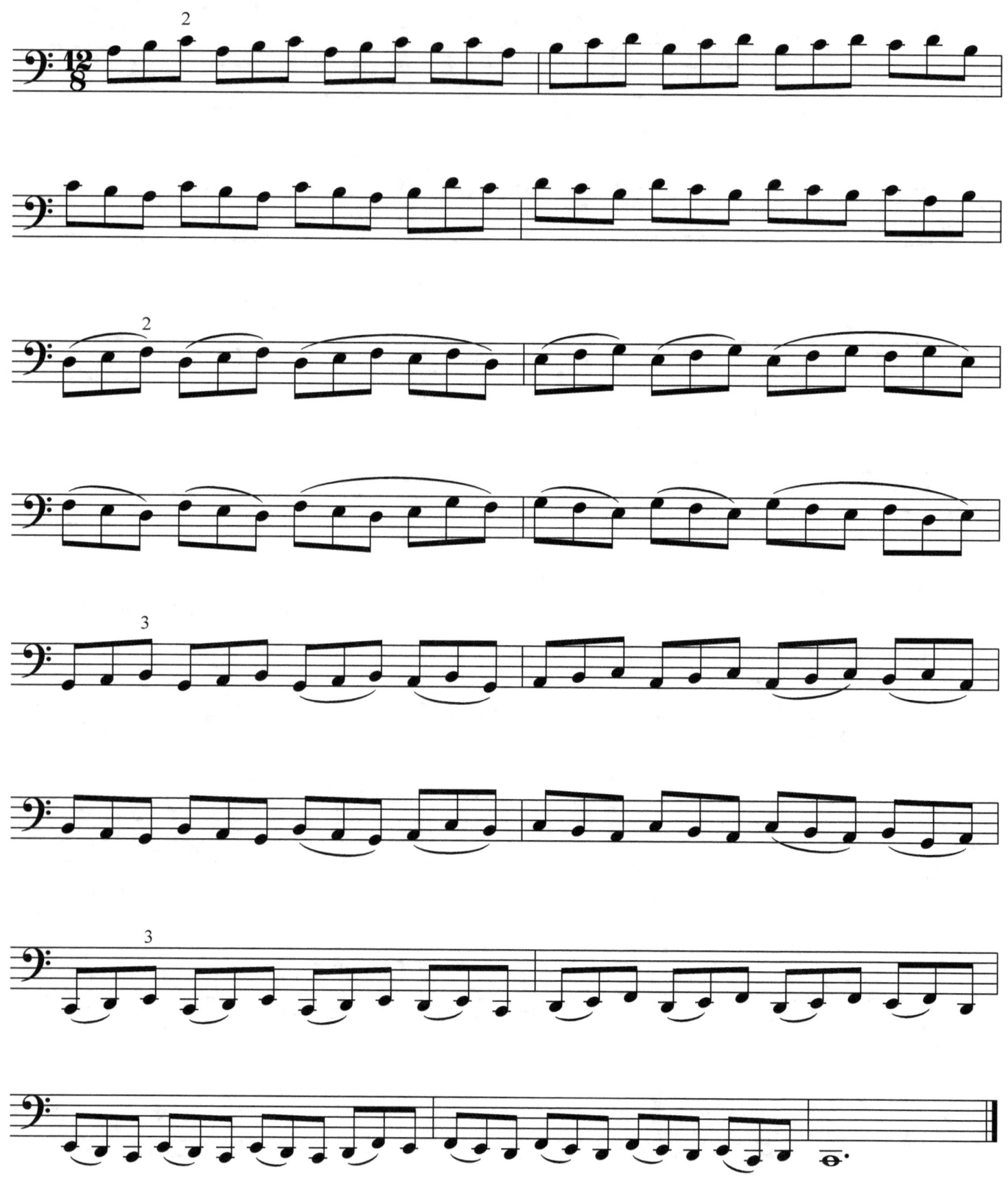

6

John James — Trad., arr. Harvey

Wicklow — Trad., arr. Harvey

7

String Crossing

8

Grenoside Sword Dance — Trad., arr. Harvey

The Mischevious Bee — Trad., arr. Harvey
(*Andante*)

9

Left-Hand Warm-Up

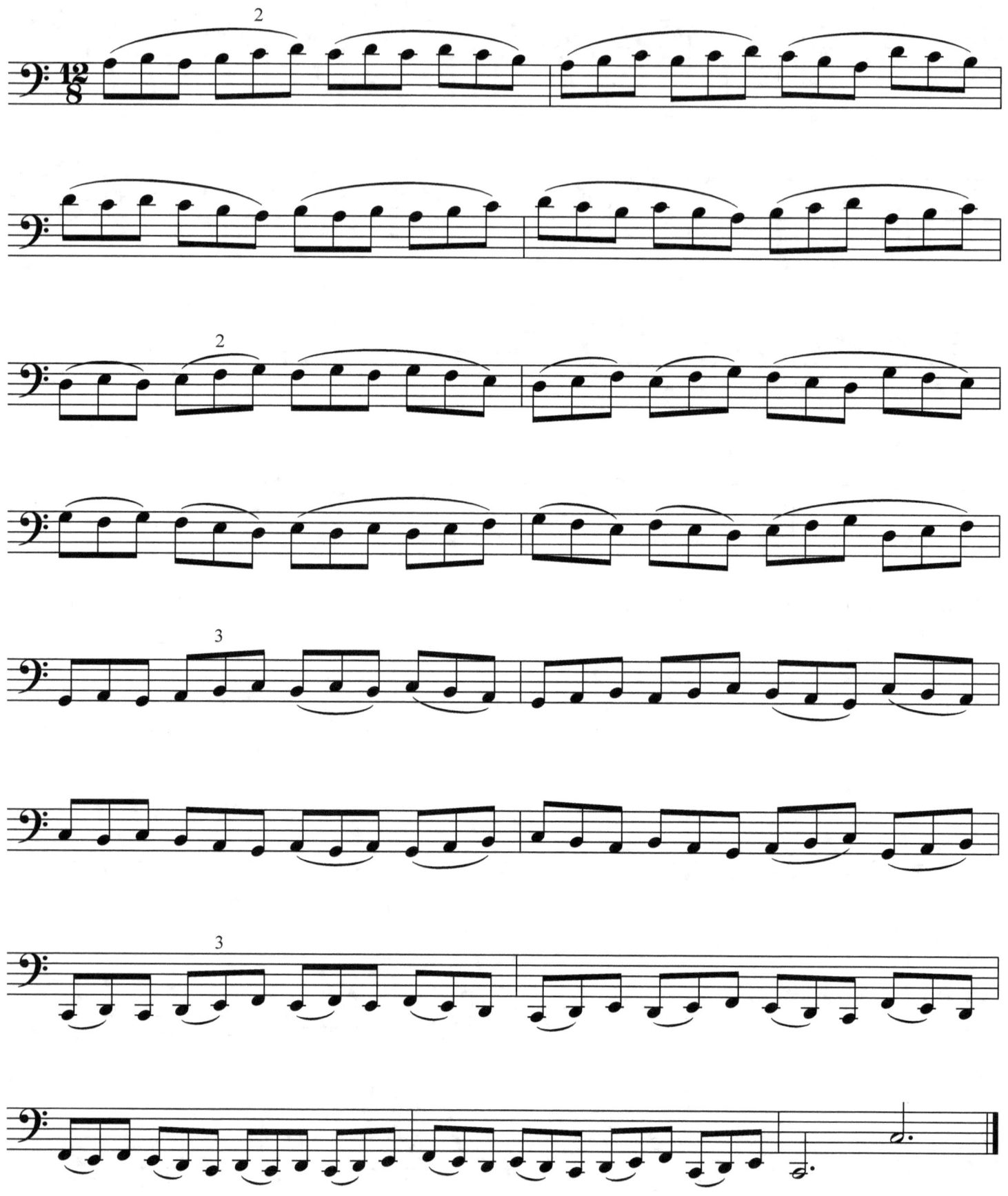

10

Warm-Up for St. Paul's Suite

St. Paul's Suite — Holst, arr. Harvey

11

String Crossing

The Triplet Book for Cello, Part One 13

12

Theme from Concerto Alla Rustica

Vivaldi, arr. Harvey

©2013 C. Harvey Publications All Rights Reserved.

13

Left-Hand Warm-Up

15

String Crossing

16

Even and Odd

Trad., arr. Harvey

17

Left-Hand Warm-Up

19

String Crossing

20

The Triplet Book for Cello, Part One

The Drum Major — Trad., arr. Harvey

Oh Dear, What Can the Matter Be — Trad., arr. Harvey

©2013 C. Harvey Publications All Rights Reserved.

21

Left-Hand Warm-Up

22

La Pastorale — Burgmuller, arr. Harvey

23

String Crossing

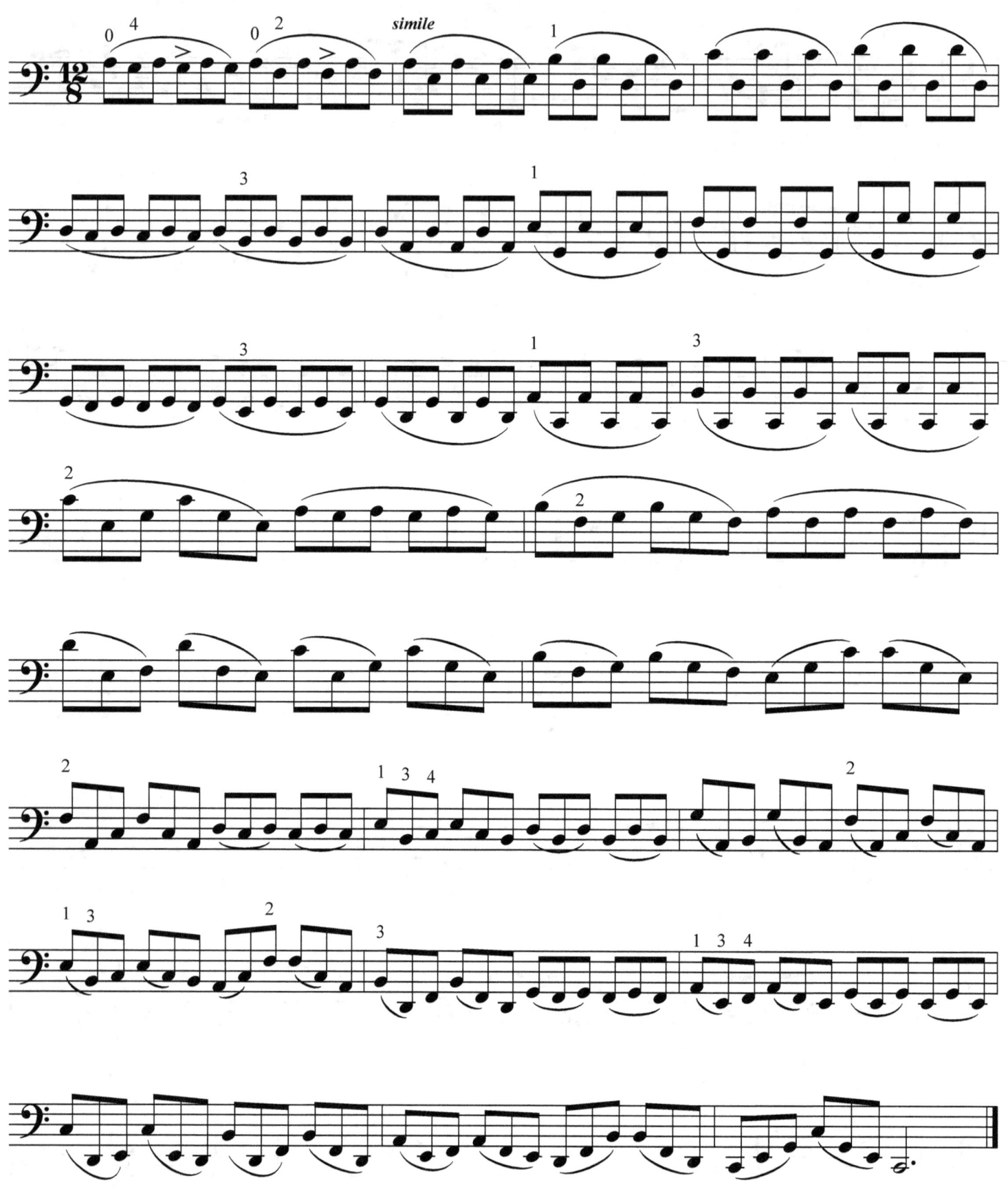

25

Left-Hand Warm-Up

The Triplet Book for Cello, Part One

26

Garry Owen — Trad., arr. Harvey

Gigue — Anon., arr. Harvey

©2013 C. Harvey Publications All Rights Reserved.

27

String Crossing

28

The Campbells are Coming — Trad., arr. Harvey

Haste to the Wedding! — Trad., arr. Harvey

©2013 C. Harvey Publications All Rights Reserved.

29

Left-Hand Warm-Up

The Triplet Book for Cello, Part One

30

Allegro

Telemann, arr. Harvey

31

String Crossing

32

Allegro from Brandenburg Concerto No. 6 Bach, arr. Harvey

33

Groups of 6

The Triplet Book for Cello, Part One

34

Brandenburg Concerto No. 3
(from the violin part)

Bach, arr. Harvey

©2013 C. Harvey Publications All Rights Reserved.

35

Groups of 6

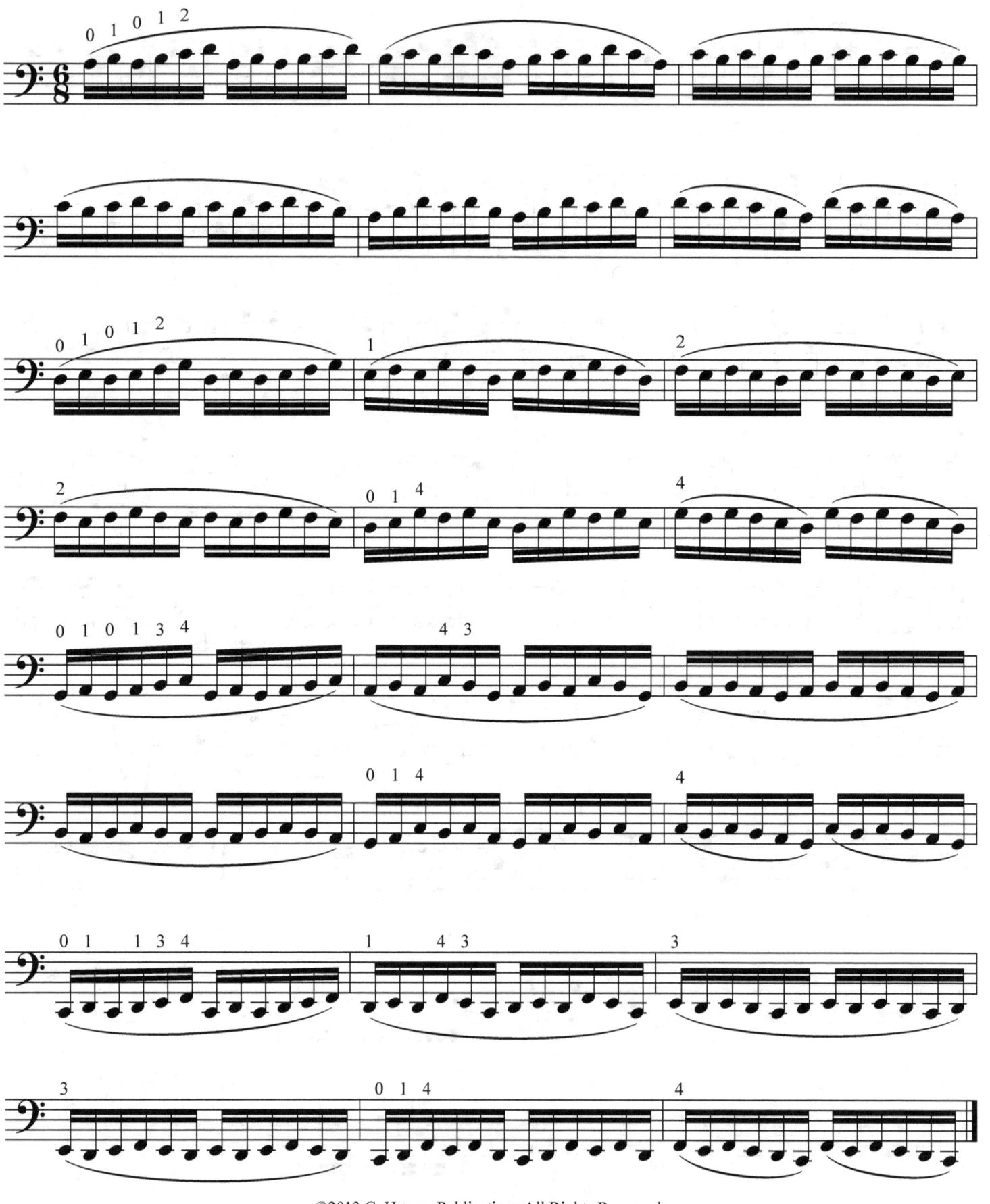

The Triplet Book for Cello, Part One

36

Albinia
Trad., arr. Harvey

37

Groups of 6

The Triplet Book for Cello, Part One

38

Lady Cholmolly's Waltz

Trad., arr. Harvey

©2013 C. Harvey Publications All Rights Reserved.

39

Groups of 6

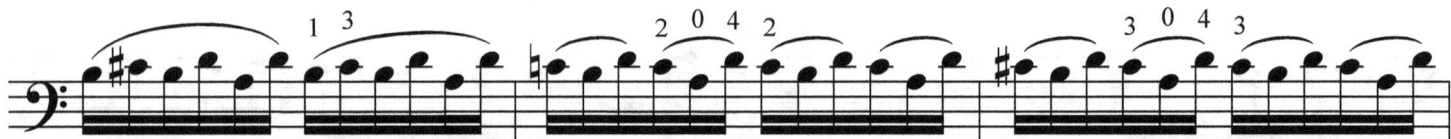

40

Over the Water — Trad., arr. Harvey

42

41

Scale Bowings

42

Gigue
Trad., arr. Harvey

43

Scale Bowings

The Triplet Book for Cello, Part One

44

Marabout　　　　　　　　　　　　　　　　　　　　　　　Anon., arr. Harvey

©2013 C. Harvey Publications All Rights Reserved.

45

Broken Thirds Bowings

46
Lord Palmerson's Favourite
The Triplet Book for Cello, Part One — Pringle, arr. Harvey

©2013 C. Harvey Publications All Rights Reserved.

47

Arpeggio Bowings

The Triplet Book for Cello, Part One

48

Off She Goes — Trad., arr. Harvey

©2013 C. Harvey Publications All Rights Reserved.

available from www.charveypublications.com:

CHP143

String Crossing; The Art of Balance

Part 1: D and G double stop

1. The first balance exercise
Cassia Harvey

Remember to change strings with your wrist and fingers,
keeping the arm and elbow balanced between two strings.

2. The first balance etude
Cassia Harvey

©2005 C. Harvey Publications All Rights Reserved

www.ingramcontent.com/pod-product-compliance
Lightning Source LLC
Chambersburg PA
CBHW051425070526
44584CB00023B/3583